T0275327

DAYS OF GRACE

Praise for *Days of Grace*:

"This down-to-earth and spiritually rich collection of meditations, prayers, and practices will speak poignantly to the hearts, minds, and souls of all those suffering from chronic, progressive, or terminal illnesses. Earle's own experience of suffering and pain makes her an authentic and compassionate guide to the far country of disease and debilitation. This brief book is a small treasure that deserves a large audience: it is in its own special way good medicine."

—Frederic and Mary Ann Brussat,
co-authors of *Spiritual Literacy* and
directors of SpiritualityandPractice.com

"Mary Earle has helped so many find a holy path through that curious daily combination of ferocity and tedium that makes up a life of chronic illness. God be thanked for the light these thoughtful essays shine on it."

—Barbara Cawthorne Crafton, author of
Jesus Wept: When Faith and Depression Meet
and *The Sewing Room: Uncommon Reflections
of Life, Love, and Work*

"Mary Earle knows that life is gift. Her words call us to the way of gratitude. Mary Earle also knows that life is gift shrouded in pain. Her words call us to the journey of grace. Both are essential. In *Days of Grace* Mary Earle wisely weaves them as one."

—John Philip Newell, author of *Christ of the
Celts: The Healing of Creation*

"This rich, wise, and comforting guide for those living with illness is a handbook of deep knowledge gleaned through lived experience. It is a blend of realism and humility, of questions and mystery—all delivered with Mary's simple yet elegant style. She unmasks many illusions and reminds us that though our lives are 'short and uncertain,' there is unfathomable power each time we realize that we have another day."

—Paula D'Arcy, author of *Gift of the Red Bird*
and *Waking Up to This Day* (2009)

DAYS OF GRACE

Meditations and Practices for Living with Illness

Mary C. Earle

Morehouse Publishing
NEW YORK · HARRISBURG · DENVER

All psalms are from The Psalter in the 1979 edition
of the Book of Common Prayer.

Morehouse Publishing, 4775 Linglestown Road,
Harrisburg, PA 17112

Morehouse Publishing, 445 Fifth Avenue,
New York, NY 10016

Morehouse Publishing is an imprint of
Church Publishing Incorporated.

Cover art courtesy of iStockphoto

Cover design by Christina Hope

Library of Congress Cataloging-in-Publication Data

Earle, Mary C.
    Days of grace : meditations and practices for living with illness /
Mary C. Earle.
        p.   cm.
    ISBN 978-0-8192-2364-7 (pbk.)
    1. Chronically ill—Prayers and devotions. 2. Sick—Prayers and
devotions. I. Title.
BV4910.E28 2009
248.8'61—dc22

                                                    2009019644

Printed in the United States of America

09 10 11 12 13 14   10 9 8 7 6 5 4 3 2 1

Dedication
For Doug, Bryan, and Jason

Contents

Acknowledgments

This work is the direct result of a question asked of me by Palmer Jones, editor of www.explorefaith.org. A couple of years ago, when we were brainstorming ideas for this website for seekers of faith in a phone conversation, she asked me if I'd write a series of meditations for persons who are living with illness. This website is aimed at anyone exploring spiritual issues, and Palmer was hoping to add to the forums and offerings. I told her that I would write the meditations, and then seized up with writer's block. Something stalled out. Palmer was patient. I was not. Then, in February 2008, a medical procedure and a brief hospitalization somehow allowed the writer's block to open, and I wrote these meditations during the ensuing recovery. Palmer waited on my timing, and received the finished work with genuine hospitality and gratitude. The meditations and practices first appeared on the explorefaith website.

The heart of this book, the meditations and practices, also exist in audio format, thanks to the creative collaboration of Elizabeth Cauthorn of Material Media, Ben Tavera King of Talking Taco Records, and Charles Garrett of Stillpoint

Studios. The talents and energies of these three brought the meditations and practices into form as MP3 files and as an audio CD.

Now, thanks to the hospitality of Church Publishing/Morehouse, the meditations and practices are also available as a book. I thank the listeners who asked repeatedly if they could have the text, and I thank Nancy Fitzgerald and the staff at Church Publishing/Morehouse, who know that in the new world of publishing, an audio format may precede the written format of a work. I am also ever grateful to Phyllis Tickle, friend and mentor, for so kindly agreeing to write the foreword.

In addition, I am indebted to the staff of Vivabooks! in San Antonio, who have so graciously promoted the audio CD, which in turn led to requests for this book.

My husband, Doug, as ever, has supported this project; his good eye led to the image chosen for the cover.

My hope is that these meditations will offer you, the reader, companionship along the journey of living with illness. You won't find answers here. Perhaps you will find that you are not walking the way of illness alone.

Foreword

Not one of us wants to be sick . . . not for a single day, thank you very much! And most certainly, not one of us wants to live out our days, or any part of them, in the grinding, relentless, compromising way that comes from having a chronic or wasting or even a terminal illness. Regardless of our own wishes and intentions, however, illness will enter the lives of more than half of us. Either we will ourselves have to suffer through a time of ill health or—and perhaps even harder to bear—those whom we love and care for will have to endure the burden and pain of illness.

No book is going to make the path through illness either smooth or desirable, but this one can render it into a thing of grace as well as into a more endurable, or possibly redemptive, burden. Perhaps just as relevant to the truth of this book is the fact that even the not-ill will find here a bouquet of understandings and insights that will sweetly scent their own, more health-blessed lives; for these pages are filled with great gifts.

It is not that all the words and sentences here are filled with startling discoveries about illness and the spiritual life. They aren't. They are suffused, instead, by realism and the humility that comes from honest engagement with it. As pages, they are also rife with startling ideas . . . not new ideas so much as old ideas re-positioned and re-imagined.

Who of us has not tossed out unthinkingly the words about our bodies being the temple of God? Yet who of us, caught in a hurting or dying body, has sought to understand that it is God's dwelling that is in pain or distress and that its Tenant and tenant are of a piece in their enduring?

Who has stopped to articulate the obvious truth that only God and the one in physical distress are able to know completely what that agony is and, then, to experience it together?

Who has seen clearly that the impotence of serious illness does not restrict the gentle heart from the action of praying for others in equal or greater difficulty, or from studying with intention upon the kindness and expertise of those who bear illness with us?

Who of us has stopped to understand that in inhabiting a sick or ailing body, God only does in particular what He already does more broadly in inhabiting an ailing creation?

And who of us—the ill or the caregivers and lovers among us—has truly realized that the gift of candor in conversation about despair authorizes the despairing to engage and often to surmount it?

Who indeed, to these and a myriad of other questions, the pivotal gift here being that the priest who speaks the words of healing in this book records them with the intimacy of one who has lived life both as priest and as sufferer. I bid your reading of what she says to your soul's health as well as to the body's relief.

Phyllis Tickle

Introduction

I'll begin at the beginning. It was a Monday in July. A hot, dry Texas summer. I had been on vacation in California, and had contracted a virus of some sort. I had a rash and felt achy. I woke up feeling tired, but had some breakfast and then sent my husband, Doug, to the office. I started feeling queasy, and within a matter of moments, I was violently ill. The onset of nausea, vomiting, acute pain took me completely by surprise. Eventually I went to the hospital in an ambulance, and was diagnosed with acute pancreatitis.

That was 1995. It's now 2009. And the episode that summer of 1995 catapulted me into the population of those who live with illness. We are many. Our lives are shaped by a variety of recurrent, chronic, progressive, or terminal illnesses. We know more about anatomy and blood chemistry than we want to. We can tell one another which doctors' waiting rooms are like holding cells in a prison and which have a humane design. Our daily rounds are often marked by clinic appointments, blood work, regimens for medications, diagnostic tests. More often than not, when we shop for food, we are scrutinizing the nutrition labels, on the alert for sugar content, fat content, or the presence of red dye. We know what it is to live within the parameters set by our illness. Our lives are formed by the requirements of these illnesses, and our days are shaped by what is needed for appropriate nutrition, rest, medication, exercise.

Our ranks are growing. As we baby boomers age, more and more of us are living with some sort of physical ailment. More and more of us are discovering that we can live *with* cancer, live *with* diabetes, live *with* heart disease. On the one hand, we are confronting the fact of human mortality. On the other, we are continually granted more days to live by the astounding progress being made in many fields of medical research. (If I'd lived in a previous generation, I would have died already from the illnesses I've had.) In this creative tension—the tension of both seeking "to number our days," and hoping that those days will be more instead of fewer—we find our life journeys intimately connected to the illnesses that we live with. I am not unique in this walk. I know many others who seek to find a way to pray, a way to discern, a way to live faithfully and compassionately while each day is marked by the presence of a physical or mental condition that has come to stay.

Our collective experience is leading many of us to question the predictable ways of responding to illness. I, for one, will be grateful if I never again hear someone suggest that an illness has been directly caused by not thinking correctly, not meditating enough, not eating whatever special diet is being touted at the moment. I also will be relieved when the Christian community renounces the tendency to assume that not getting well means that you are not living in a state of grace. These particular ways of arbitrarily assigning meaning to illness range from the punitive to the coercive, with all kinds of variations in between: "You got breast cancer because you did not love yourself as a woman." "We keep praying for you; why aren't you getting well?"

My own sense of the matter is that our culture's rush to interpret and to apply pat descriptors to the mysterious encounter with illness, reveals our deep unease with the fact of mortality. In Western culture we are particularly plagued with an inability to enter honestly and regularly into awareness of our own mortality. And so when illness appears, and a friend or a family member or a public figure endures the diminishment of treatment or surgery or rehabilitation, a whole babble of voices begins: "It happened because he just did not take care of himself." "Well, you know, God must want her to be a saint if God gave her this illness."

Such responses also call into question our latent images of God. The last thing those of us who live with illness need is one more punitive image of God. And yet often that is what is served up: "God is testing you through this illness." "God must want you to love him more, so he gave your son this cancer." "God needs another angel, so you will be helping him when you die."

Oh, please.

Surely we can find a more sane, more compassionate way of speaking and praying with one another when illness appears. Surely we can invite a kindly awareness, something that mirrors what the ancient Israelites called *chesed*, the steadfast love of God, the love that will not let us go, the mercy that is all-encompassing. When we are ill, when our nights are plagued by anxious thoughts and by the sheer fact of our numbered days, when we know in our bones that the next doctor's appointment will reveal that the cancer is back, we need the deep reassurance of the steadfast love of God. We need the constant, faithful reminder that the God who makes us is the same God who holds us in being and will receive us at our life's end. We need the deep consolation that God will not leave us alone, even when we may be solitary. We desire the quiet affirmation that God knit us together in our mother's womb, and that there is no darkness that is dark to God. We yearn to be reminded: "Fear not."

I have written these meditations as an offering for those of us who live with illness. My hope is that as you pray them, as you engage the practices, you will encounter gentle possibilities for discovering God's presence with you in and through all that you endure. Please use the meditations at your own pace. And if you find a particular meditation or practice that does not speak to you, just skip over it. By the same token, if a meditation or practice tugs at your attention for a few days, or even a few weeks, allow yourself the gift of staying with that part of the text as long as it speaks to you. In a way, the meditations are spiritual food. Allow them to be a kind of nutrition, taking them in at a pace that allows them to be digested gently. Don't rush. Don't feel pressured to "finish." If and when something calls to you in the text, stop and listen. Allow heart and soul and body to quiet, to be open to the Voice that is within you, seeking to make known the merciful and gentle Presence that hallows every trip to the doctor's office, every hospitalization, every diagnostic procedure.

The Psalms

You will notice that each of the meditations begins with a line from the psalms. In part, this is because the psalms have been an integral part of my daily prayer life for almost thirty years. I have begun each day with a psalm, and then taken the line or phrase that caught my attention, and journaled about that line as a form of prayer.

As a consequence, when I became ill, the psalms were already my natural habitat of prayer. The voice that one finds in the psalms brings all of human feeling to speech: joy, rage, delight, anxiety, fear, peace, hope, concern. Praying the psalms had taught me that this book of Scripture gives us explicit models for being completely honest and vulnerable in our prayer life. The ancient Israelites included both personal and communal lament in their book of Psalms, and when we are living with illness, we will find verses that state for us the deep distress and the confusion we are likely to be experiencing. And the psalms give us a means of praying when we find, to our utter surprise, that the cancer is in remission, the blood sugar is within normal limits, the heart bypass worked. The psalms offer both a way of naming the times when we are in the "pit" and the times when we are set free to hope.

The psalms, as more than one commentator has observed, appear to have been Jesus' way of prayer. More often than not, a verse of a psalm is on his lips. At one point in my life, I thought this might have been contrived by the communities that kept the stories of Jesus alive and eventually produced the gospels. Now, after praying for years with the psalms, I know how often a line from a psalm will come to my awareness in all kinds of situations. The psalms are part of me; they shape my daily prayer and as a consequence, they have given me words for times of deep distress, occasions fraught with grief and anxiety, moments when I felt I was at the end of my rope. I have found verses in the psalms that have spoken into being a new lightness of heart, a barely dawning hope, a vulnerable rebirth of trust. This language has become part of me, and so in writing the meditations, the psalms were the primary touchstone for each meditation and practice.

So, we will begin each of these meditations with a psalm, joining a tradition at least three thousand years old. We are joining our voices, our hearts and souls, to those of many others who have voiced these words, first in Hebrew, then in Greek, then in Latin, then in every language across the globe. Our prayer of the psalm verse, like a little running creek, joins the great river of prayer swelling through time and space.

The Meditations and Practices

In the layout of this book, you will note that each meditation begins with a line from a psalm. You may have occasions when that one line is sufficient food for the day. The words before you on the page may cause you to awaken to a new perception, to ponder something new about yourself or about God, to stop and savor or wonder. The layout is intended to give you explicit permission to ingest the lines from the psalms, and the meditations, at a gentle, easy pace. You may even find that you put the book down for several weeks and then return to it when you are ready.

My intent, with the gracious collaboration of my editor and the graphic design team, is to offer you a sense of freedom and gentleness when you are reading this book. So often when living with illness, we find that we do not have control over much of anything. While that is true of life in general, it is also the case that in coping with the regimens of illness, one's whole identity can seem to be subsumed in an overwhelming array of medical procedures that often seem like a kind of job. My hope is that this text will offer invitation and hospitality, but never a sense of your being force-fed.

That said, I have also been told by some who listened to the meditations and practices in the audio format that they listened all the way through the first time, not stopping to practice, and then began again, reading and praying the mediations, one step at a time. Their second journey through the text unfolded slowly, with lots of time for each meditation and practice. You will find the pace that works for you. And, you can always double back, beginning again, if for some reason returning to the beginning seems to be the path you need to take.

Each meditation is inspired directly by the verse from the psalm. Sometimes the meditation is anecdotal. Sometimes it is reflective. Sometimes it is provocative. The meditations are not sequential; if you want to dip into them without following the numerical order, go right ahead. You may discover that a particular meditation is good for you on the day of checkup, or another upon preparing to go to the hospital. You might want to use sticky notes to mark these, so that they are readily available as you put the book in your suitcase or tote bag or purse. Its size is intended to enhance its portability, so that the meditations and practices may go with you wherever you go.

The Practices

The practices are offered as a way of deepening and claiming the awareness offered in the meditations. They are truly *practices*—something suggested for you to do in response to the psalm verse and the meditation. And as with any practice, whether that be playing the piano or throwing a ball or knitting, returning to the practice allows it to become more of a habit. Because I am a writer, much of what I suggest invites a written response. You will need to have writing materials at hand, preferably a simple notebook and whatever pen or marker or pencil you wish to use. I am aware that for some, writing will not be possible, and in the course of the practices, I've offered other possibilities if that is the case.

As with the meditations, so with the practices. Go at your own pace. Recently I received an e-mail from a woman who had been using the audio format of *Days of Grace*. One particular practice had caught her attention, and she had returned to it many times in the course of a month. I hope that every reader will use the practices in the way that is of most benefit to her or him.

"The Place of My Resurrection"

In the received tradition from Celtic Christianity (from the lands of Scotland, Ireland, Wales, Cornwall, Brittany, the Isle of Man, Galicia) we find many stories of the Celtic saints who enacted a particular kind of pilgrimage. Rather than following a set route, heading toward an announced destination such as Rome or Jerusalem, the Celtic saints followed a different pattern. After prayer and self-dedication, they got into a small boat called a coracle. This coracle was made by bending strips of wood into a bowl shape, and then sealing leather over the wood with tar. A coracle (or *curragh*) looks like a big bowl. There are no oars.

Think about that: a boat that looks like a bowl. With no oars.

In Celtic practice, you got in the boat, and entrusted yourself to "the currents of love," which meant the currents of the sea or the river. You got into the boat and you let go. You got into the boat and you physically cast yourself on the mercy and love of God.

The coracle would spin and drift on the currents until at last it was brought to shore. And the tradition says that the place of arrival is "the place of my resurrection." The place of arrival is that place that Love has brought us to.

In a way, living with illness is akin to getting in the coracle. We have to let go of all kinds of expectations and scripts we may have had for our lives. We have to float on the currents of Love in the midst of interruptions, diminishments, physical impairment, weakness, relational tensions. And yet the coracle of our lives is borne along, whether the coracle is navigating white water and cataracts or has come into a calm expanse.

In the reality and the metaphor of the coracle, we see a people and a practice that trusts in the love and mercy of God. We see a trust that is willing to leave the outcome and the destination in God's hand. This kind of pilgrimage is also a pilgrimage toward Home. The Celtic saints understood "the place of my resurrection" both to be the place where I will die, and the place where I will return to the God who knit me together in my mother's womb. The wandering saints, as they were called, set forth understanding that we are in this life always as *hospites mundi*, guests of the world. We live in this world not of our own making. We are here for numbered days, and we are here both to bless and to enjoy the world God has created. Our earthly life truly is transitory. And it is a gift, even when it is marked by illness.

The Celtic saints, in this practice of getting into the coracle, offer those of us living with illness a way through. The illness becomes like a coracle, and we know that most of the time we don't have oars—and we don't have control. Some days we know in our very cells that we are borne along by God's mercy. Other days we won't be so sure. And some days will be marked by total numbness and shock as we adjust to new difficulties. Entrusting the coracle of our life to God's grace and mercy, we persevere and we endure. And yet there are days of grace. And there is light in the darkness.

My hope is that these meditations and practices will invite you to discern your own days and times of grace, and to know that the steadfast love of the God who makes, redeems, and sustains you will ever be in you—heart, body, and soul.

DAY ONE

You will show me the path of life.

Psalm 16:11

If you are reading this meditation, in all probability you are learning to live with illness. Your illness may be chronic or progressive or terminal. Whatever the case, you are entering a school of experience for which our culture offers little wisdom. You are seeking to find a way to live with the stresses and the discomforts of a body that is somehow weakened. You are trying to live within new limitations. You are also coming face-to-face with the fact of your own mortality.

The wisdom tradition of Scripture tells us that this kind of experience, as harsh and painful as it may be, also offers us the opportunity to come to terms with reality. We begin to remember that we are creatures. We begin to recognize that our lives are fragile and that our bodies can suffer from many different maladies. We begin to reorient and reframe our lives, within a new context— a context of difficult days and unexpected physical disruption. And we may begin to ask deeper questions about meaning and about life, about death and about eternity. When we ask those questions, we are beginning to take the first steps on a path of life. We are beginning to live at a deeper level, though it may not be the path we would have chosen had illness not intervened.

Prayer

Gracious God, in whom I live and move and have my being, as I learn to live with this illness, may I be open to your presence and mercy.
Amen.

Practice

For these practices, have your notebook and pen on hand.

1. Write down questions that have arisen for you as a result of living with illness. Be honest. No one else will read what you've written.
2. Choose one question to hold quietly in prayer. Write the question on a piece of paper. Place the paper in your hands, then hold your hands together in a receptive gesture. Offer your question in prayer, saying "I offer this question to You in love, O God." Or use a prayer of your own.
3. Continue with this practice as you feel God is leading you. There's no need to rush.
4. Make note of what occurs to you as you sit with the question. You might become aware of your own feelings or memories, uncertainties or frustrations. Gently allow yourself to receive what comes to your notice.
5. Bring the practice to a close with a simple prayer of thanksgiving.

DAY TWO

Have pity on me, O LORD.

Psalm 9:13

When illness has come to live within your life—
not as a guest, but as a permanent resident—you
may feel singled out. We have inherited a strange
and punitive way of thinking about illness. Often
we are told that being sick is our fault. If we had
only eaten the right food, meditated sufficiently, or
been less anxious, we would not have become ill.

On one level this is true. If I have smoked two
packs of cigarettes a day for years, I have compromised my lungs, and it is more likely that I will
develop lung cancer. If I have overindulged in

alcohol for most of my life, I might develop some malady of the liver. And then again, I might not.

On a deeper level, there is no simple formula for cause and effect when it comes to living with illness. The fact is that all bodies eventually fail. Bodies wear out. The inner processes of cell division can go awry. The amazing capacities for transformation of food into energy can be disrupted. We all eventually die.

The assurance that our tradition and experience offers is this: whatever suffering and disorientation the illness has brought, God is present in and through that suffering and disorientation. In the words of Paul Claudel, "Jesus did not come to explain away suffering or remove it. He came to fill it with his presence."

Prayer

God of Mercy, grant me eyes to see and ears to hear, that I may recognize your presence in Christ through every hard passage as I live with this illness.

Amen.

Practice

Using your journal, start a running list of moments when you have known the presence of God in and through your illness. Possible times of knowing that mercy of presence might include: through the skill of doctors and nurses, through the prayers of family and friends, through deep silence in the midst of recovery. Return to this list from time to time, especially when you are feeling abandoned or neglected by God. Add to the list as you are led.

DAY THREE

❧

Surely, you behold trouble and misery;
you see it and take it into your own hand.

Psalm 10:14

We live in a culture of the quick fix. If we have a diagnosis that is not likely to result in that quick fix, we can find ourselves at odds with dominant perspectives, even within our faith community. I have lived with chronic pancreatitis since 1995, and I have recently had my eighth endoscopic microsurgery. There are no quick fixes for this condition. There are no ready solutions.

Many who are reading these words find themselves in the same sort of dilemma. Perhaps you find yourself yearning, as we all do, for some miracle cure. Perhaps you find yourself wanting God

23

to intervene in a miraculous way. I have certainly had those desires.

And yet, the peculiarity of my own anatomy that creates the chronic condition remains the same. God in Christ indwells the not-perfect creation that is my body, just as God in Christ indwells the not-perfect creation of the whole universe. God does behold the trouble and the misery. Before God we are never invisible, never unseen, never ignored. Our trouble and misery are seen and known for what they are—trouble and misery. God meets us in that deep distress, even when we cannot sense God's presence.

Prayer

In the deep distress of living with this illness, may I know that You behold every moment of pain and fear. May I know that You are with me.

Amen.

Practice

In your journal, write down a description of the illness that you live with. If, for example, you live with a heart condition, you might write, "My heart is weakened and has lost its ability to pump blood efficiently." Be specific. Then allow yourself to become quiet and receptive. Breathing gently and slowly, place your hands on what you have written, and pray the prayer offered at the end of this meditation: *In the deep distress of living with this illness, may I know that You behold every moment of pain and fear. May I know that You are with me. Amen.* Let your hands connect the description of the illness to the prayer, the imperfection to the yearning for God's presence.

NOTE: If you cannot write, and you wish to keep a record, you could record your responses with a mini–tape recorder. If that is not an option that is right for you, feel free to disregard the directives about writing, and to mentally follow the suggestions. Alternatively, if you have a trusted friend who might track the practices with you, he or she might be your scribe.

Also, if at any time a practice seems unsuitable for your condition or your present spiritual, emotional, and psychological state, skip it.

DAY FOUR

※❀※

Hear the voice of my prayer
when I cry out to you.

Psalm 28:2

Living with illness gives us a strange gift. When
we live with a body that is compromised in some
way, we discover our need of others and our need
of God. It is a gift to discover this need, though it
may be completely disconcerting.

Most of us are socialized to be self-sufficient
and independent. Acknowledging that we are each
a part of a vast, interdependent web of life may
be a completely new perspective. And yet it is the
truth. None of us is truly self-sufficient. None of
us brought ourselves into being.

In the words of C. S. Lewis, there is a "severe mercy" that is offered in living with illness.[1] Our illusions of not needing one another fall apart. We may need help walking or need a friend to help us with errands. We may need financial support. We may need someone to talk to. And in that awareness of our need, we come upon this truth: we are contingent beings, dependent on God for our life and our relationships.

Awakening to this brings us to deeper prayer. We cry out to God, asking for healing, asking for companions in the pilgrimage of illness, asking for release from pain. In the crying out, we allow ourselves to be honest and vulnerable, and something new can begin. Living with illness may grant us the severe mercy of becoming real.

Prayer

For this day, this moment, may I cry out the desires of my heart. May I trust that You will hear every groan, every sigh, every tear.

Amen.

Practice

Reflect on the phrase "severe mercy." What severe mercies have you experienced as a result of your illness? Make note of them as they occur to you. If there are as yet no mercies in your experience, note that as well. Be honest with yourself and take that honesty into prayer.

Day Five

I will bless the LORD at all times;
his praise shall ever be in my mouth.

Psalm 34:1

How to live with illness? How to find a path of life in the midst of treatment, procedures, blood work, and hospitalizations? How to find a practice of prayer when our illness itself keeps us so busy—and often so discouraged?

Some years ago, when I was visiting an older parishioner in a hospital, Joanna told me that in the night, when she could not sleep, she made a practice of praying for everyone in the hospital. She would ask God to bless each patient and family member, each doctor, each nurse, each nurse's assistant, each janitor, each cook, each lab tech. I remember being taken aback by her capacity to pray for others in the midst of her own distress.

Joanna was in her eighties, and she had a great gift for intercessory prayer. She was speaking from the fruit of her life experience, from her own experience of diminishment and increasing pain. "I bless God by asking God to bless all these others," she explained. "We are all connected, you know." She said this with her typical Joanna-smile, and with the authority of a woman who had been a teacher for most of her life.

This day, allow yourself the space and time to ask God's blessing on those who live with the same illness that afflicts you. Ask God's blessing on the researchers who create medicines and treatments that allow you to live with the illness. And remember especially those who have no access to medical care. In remembering them, we bless God who blesses us.

Prayer

Gracious God of Life and Mercy, grant me the awareness of others who live with illness. Teach

me to pray for those who care for and tend the
sick. And may my prayers bless You.

Amen.

Practice

Write down the names of other people you know
who live with the same ailment that you do. If
you live with something rare and don't know of
others who live with this illness, just write down
something that helps you remember that there are
others who have the same malady. For today, be
intentional about praying for others who live with
the same illness that you live with. Light a candle.
Send a check to those who research cures for the
illness. Or, if you are able and willing, find a way
to embody the intercession through action—if
you have received radiation, take good magazines
to the radiation center. If you are receiving kidney
dialysis, remember to take appropriate snacks to
the waiting area. There are many ways to offer
prayer for one another; you will no doubt come
up with a creative embodiment of your prayer.

DAY SIX

*LORD, let me know my end and
the number of my days, so that
I may know how short my life is.*

Psalm 39:5

Several years ago, after I had been in the hospital, my husband and I took a driving trip to New Mexico. We savored the stunning scenery of the high road from Santa Fe to Taos, and then followed a big circle through the landscape, stopping at various sites along the way. The ancient rock and open space gave me an unexpected grace—a sense of my own littleness and of the shortness of human life. Those mountains have been there for eons, and have witnessed the passing of many generations.

For some reason, at that moment, it was truly good news to me to recognize the brevity of human life. Even if I were to live to be ninety, in contrast to the endurance of the mountains, that is just the blink of an eye.

And from the perspective of eternity, from the eternal *now* that is God's time outside of time, our lives are brief.

The ancient Hebrews knew this truth better than we do today. Much in our culture leads us to participate in the illusion that we will live forever, that none of us will fall ill, that tragedy will never strike as long as we "do the right thing." We need the medicine of remembering that our lives are short and uncertain, contingent and interdependent. And oddly enough, living with illness helps us remember those truths.

Prayer

Gentle Christ, you brought me into being and sustain my earthly life. May I know that my numbered days are sustained by your love and that I will be received into the arms of mercy at my end. Amen.

Practice

Practice: In your journal, write "Teach me to number my days, that I may apply my heart to wisdom" (a variation on Ps. 90:12). Then begin noting in writing what kinds of wisdom, insight, and common sense you have been awakened to as a result of living with illness. Return to the list from time to time, both to add to it and to reflect. You may want to put the list in a place where it is readily visible—on a mirror or the inside cover of your journal. Give thanks for the wisdom that living with illness brings.

DAY SEVEN

⚜

"A deadly thing," they say,
"has fastened on him."

Psalm 41:8

Years ago as a seminarian I had the happy experience of being mentored by the Rev. Charles Meyer at St. David's Hospital in Austin, Texas. Chuck was something of an iconoclast. He insisted that we as a society, and as a people of faith, needed to explicitly acknowledge that we were mortal and that dying would happen to all of us. He did not have much patience with the seminarians who distanced themselves from patients in the hospital, essentially saying, "A deadly thing has fastened on him." Chuck taught with humor and story.

He also taught by example and deed as much as by speech. He often said, "Never bury someone until they are dead." Sometimes when we are living with illness, we will deal with friends and family who inadvertently begin to treat us as if we were not fully alive. Even when we are in hospice care, we are still not dead. Even when a disease has claimed mobility and mental faculty, we have a sacred personhood in Christ.

Notice the persons who help you remember that you are alive. Notice the friends and acquaintances, caregivers and doctors whose engagement with you offers companionship along the way of illness. Give thanks for them and remember to thank them for the gift of receiving your life, however marked by illness it may be—receiving your life as *life*, singular, sacred, and true.

Prayer

I give You thanks, most gracious God, for those who have helped me along the way. I ask for wisdom in responding to those who can only say "a deadly thing has fastened on you." And I give

You thanks for leading me to see the varieties of life
I have known through this illness.
Amen.

Practice

Write down the names of those who have helped
you remember that your life is singular, sacred,
and true. Give thanks specifically for each of these
persons. As you are led, write each person, by
e-mail or by snail mail, to let them know of your
gratitude. Be specific in naming the gift that you
have received from them—a kindness, a steady
presence, a gift of food or good reading material,
or perhaps monetary support. Return to this practice from time to time, remembering those who
have given you the gift of blessing your life.

DAY EIGHT

⁂

*I call upon you from the ends of the earth
with heaviness in my heart.*

Psalm 61:2

Living with illness leads us to pray with honesty.
We learn to pray in and through the details of test
results and the loneliness of deep fatigue. With
chronic, progressive, or terminal illness, we sometimes bump headlong into a passage that makes
our hearts heavy. It may be one test too many. It
may be a development that requires another hospitalization. It may be the sheer grind of living
with the demands of illness.

The psalms tell us to pray the heaviness of
heart. Don't gussy it up. Don't try to make it

pretty. Bring the heaviness of heart to speech. If you are sad, pray the sadness. If you are feeling hard-pressed, pray that feeling. If you are feeling besieged by diagnostic procedures, name that sense of being besieged.

True prayer begins with this honest vulnerability. Bring your heaviness of heart to your prayer, trusting that God in Christ is meeting you there, receiving all the pain and the frustration, the fear and the anxiety. Remember that God is with you, as close as your breath, as near as your heartbeat.

Prayer

Ever-gentle Christ, my heart is sore and heavy with all that this illness has brought into my life. Be with me in my daily life; be with all who live with this illness in their lives.

Amen.

Practice

For this practice, you will need some space and time for quiet reflection. Read the suggestion all the way through, then do the relaxation and meditation. Afterward you may wish to write in your journal.

Begin by breathing gently in a position that is comfortable for your condition. Allow your breath to find its own gentle rhythm. As you breathe in, allow yourself to become aware of God's gentle presence in the breath itself. As you breathe out, let go of tension. Focus gently on the breath.

Once your breath has established its rhythm, add this prayer silently to the breath:

Heal and restore (inhalation),
my heavy heart (exhalation).

Try initially to pray in this way for five to ten minutes. Don't force anything. If this prayer doesn't work for you, try creating one that names your feelings. Return to this breath prayer from time to time so that it may deepen within you.

If you wish, you may want to journal about this time of prayer, noting what comes to your attention, and how (or if) you notice changes in your own feelings of sadness, frustration, or anxiety. The prayer is not magic; the prayer is a means of naming your honest feelings within the kindly encircling of God's mercy.

DAY NINE

For God alone my soul in silence waits.

Psalm 62:1

Living with illness sometimes offers us silence. We may become homebound when formerly we went to a workplace. We may experience the particular silence of a hospital at night, when another person is dying just down the hall. We may discover that our prayer inclines more and more toward silence, for our speech cannot carry the weight of our experience.

Thomas Keating, Trappist monk and teacher of centering prayer, has said that "silence is God's first language."[2] If you find yourself being drawn toward silence and stillness in prayer, trust that longing. Our Christian tradition offers the wisdom that at our deepest core, we abide in the rich, creative silence of God. At our deepest core, beyond the daily realities of the illness, Christ dwells in you and you dwell in Christ. In that space within, where your embodied life is grounded and rooted in Love, the silence of Mercy awaits.

Today, take the time to choose silence and stillness. Take the time to rest in the God who creates you at this moment and who will receive you at your end. Allow yourself to rest in the silent Presence who will never leave you and will ever be your friend.

Prayer

Grant me, gracious God, the space and time to rest in You, to know your presence in silence and to know your love that makes me, keeps me, and receives me.

Amen.

Practice

A regular practice of silent resting prayer is supported by finding the place that will allow you to inhabit the silence. This could be a chair, or your bed, or a place outdoors. You may know immediately which place will allow you to step into a practice of silence. Or you may need to try out different places to see how each one feels.

Once you have found the right place, try to allow yourself to sit or lie quietly. Allow your attention to rest on the rhythm of your breath. This kind of silence is akin to that moment just before sleep descends—a kind of letting go, a kind of entrusting. If you become drowsy, don't worry about it. This silence is set aside for us to remember what it is to rest in the presence of God. This silence is not focused attention. Breathe and rest. If you need words, just say, "Thank You," and leave it at that.

Return to silent resting prayer as often as you wish.

DAY TEN

❧❦❧

*I will dwell in your house forever; I will
take refuge under the cover of your wings.*

Psalm 61:4

Living with illness is all the more difficult if
I am struggling with a punitive image of God. If
I have a notion that God decided to strike me with
a malady, it will be very difficult to sense that God
is merciful. If I have been brought up to believe that
God has nothing better to do than find mean ways
to hurt people, I am not likely to trust that Creator.

In a strange way, living with illness often
unmasks our latent images of God. We discover
that we may harbor suspicions that God has singled us out for punishment via cancer or multiple

sclerosis or heart disease. If you have found these kinds of thoughts in your own reflection, they need to be seen for what they are—illusion.

The ongoing witness of Scripture and tradition assures us that God is gracious and compassionate. God's own house is known for hospitality and welcome, not mean-spirited action. The psalmist offers us an image as tender as a mother bird, under whose wings we might shelter. As you pray through your own life with illness, allow yourself to notice how you picture God. If those images and pictures fill you with dread and cowering fear, they need to be ditched.

Allow yourself to dwell in the steadfast love of God's own house, to seek shelter under the gentle wing of mercy.

Prayer

Merciful and loving Christ, help me to know You as You are. Grant me a sure sense of your presence and guidance, that as I walk with this illness, I may know that your love is steadfast.

Amen.

Practice

Sit or lie in a comfortable position. Gently focus your attention on your breath. As you begin to enter the prayer, offer these words:

I will take refuge in You.

Repeat the phrase silently, noticing what the phrase evokes for you. Stay with this repetition for as long as you wish. When you are ready, relinquish the words. Focus on the breath. Offer silent thanksgiving. You may wish to journal about your prayer.

DAY ELEVEN

❦

You have gone up on high and
led captivity captive.

Psalm 68:18

What holds you captive? I can say, quite truly, that pancreatitis has held me captive. It is true that since 1995 the condition has been a formative force in my life. Because of chronic pancreatitis I took a medical retirement at age fifty-five. Because of pancreatitis I haven't had butter, bacon, or a glass of wine in thirteen years.

Yet living with illness has led me to discover various other captivities. For instance, I am one of many Americans who succumbed to collapsing my identity into work. I was captive to the script,

"I am what I do." I also learned that I was captive to my own assumptions of middle-class privilege. For example, I have decent health insurance and a disability retirement plan. While those are great mercies for me, I realize now I was captive to being so self-focused I was not mindful of the needs of others—all those others who have no health-care coverage or disability insurance. All those others for whom the costs of prescriptions and hospitalization are prohibitive.

The captivity of an illness may lead captivity captive. In other words, the very limitations we live with may set us free. We may discover an unexpected freedom that delivers us from being excessively self-focused. It may, in time, release us from our blindness to the lack of services to others in our communities, in our nation, and in the world. Living with illness and the consequent limitations may offer us the freeing grace of compassion and kindness. The strange truth is that our illness may be the agent of liberation from selfishness and from blindness to the needs of others.

Prayer

Gracious God, through this illness may You lead my captivities captive. May You release me into the freedom of being deeply mindful of my neighbor. May You use this illness to lead me into compassion and generosity, remembering that You are always leading us out of slavery into freedom.

Amen.

Practice

The next time you are waiting in a doctor's office, notice the other persons who are there. Silently pray, "May the Christ in me bless the Christ in you," as you behold each face. Allow yourself to notice other patients, lab techs, nurses, receptionists, bookkeepers, doctors. Gently, silently, sustain the prayer. If you are so inclined, let this become your prayer practice in every waiting room—a quiet, reflective offering, hid with Christ in the midst of the activity of the clinic, treatment center, or lab facility.

DAY TWELVE

⁂

I am sinking in deep mire,
and there is no firm ground for my feet.

Psalm 69:2

In 2004 our thirty-year-old son Bryan was diagnosed with a kind of brain cancer called astrocytoma. He lived for sixteen months with this cancer, enduring surgery, radiation, and chemotherapy. At one point in 2005, the radiation created swelling in the brain that led to grand mal seizures. Bryan lived with the seizures and with the hospitalizations. He had a twenty-four-hour brain scan that left him sleepless and disoriented.

When he came home, he collapsed in tears. He was "sinking in mire." He was exhausted by the cancer, by the constant treatment, by the lack of sleep. He felt there was "no firm ground." The most faithful act he could offer was falling apart. Bryan was beyond trying to be strong. His prayer was the complete and faithful embodiment of exhaustion and desperation.

The fact is that there are moments like this for those of us living with illness. We sense that the ground has given way beneath us. We lose our orientation. We feel deep sadness and fear. And it seems that there is no light shining in the darkness.

Allow yourself the truth of these moments. Do not gloss over them. Bryan had family and friends who held him and listened to him in his despair. Not all who live with illness have those kinds of resources. Bryan lost his footing. The path he eventually found in the aftermath of the seizures was very different than the path he'd previously been on. Bryan began to prepare for his death.

Prayer

Merciful and loving Christ, at times I lose my footing. At times I feel I cannot bear up under

*the duress of this illness. Sustain me in my sadness
and fear, in my exhaustion and grief. Encircle me
with your love.*

Amen.

Practice

Have you lost your footing at times when living
with illness? What has that been like? How have
you regained footing—if indeed you have? If not,
what shape has your life taken? Reflect on these
questions, and, if you wish, take the time to write
your responses in your journal. It may be that you
can't find words to articulate the loss of footing.
You may simply want to sit in silence, or you
may find that there is a deep sadness that needs
accompaniment.

If you need the partnership of a friend or a
medical professional as you reflect on this aspect
of living with illness, you may want to defer
the practice until you can tell another of your
experience.

Be mindful that your mercy for yourself is always held in God's mercy. If you find yourself in despair, know that others have also encountered despair.

Including Jesus.

DAY THIRTEEN

Answer me, O LORD, for your love is kind;
in your great compassion, turn to me.

Psalm 69:18

We all want answers. One of my ways of dealing with the mysterious aspects of illness is to get more information. While knowledge can be helpful, it won't necessarily provide answers. Our bodies are amazing creations, and while modern medicine is pretty amazing, it is still more of an art than a science. My grandfather was a physician, and he was fond of saying, "Medicine is an inexact science."

When I had my first attack of acute pancreatitis in 1995, the search for *why* began. I had blood tests. I had CT scans and MRIs. The doctor took a complete medical history. And to this day, we don't really know why these attacks started. Yes, I'd had a bad virus the week before, and sometimes a virus will trigger an attack. Yes, blood tests revealed that I had high triglycerides so that could be the source. And yes, there was that anomaly—that anatomical glitch.

I almost drove myself nuts trying to find an answer. Then I realized that what I was really trying to find was a cure. In and of itself, that is not a bad thing. However, my search for an answer kept leading me from living my new life. Yes, I'd ended up with a different life—a life whose boundaries had been enclosed by an illness. In a startling way, letting go of the need for an answer allowed my soul to heal.

A wise physician said to me, "Try to find a balance. Live your life before you lose it. And let yourself know that you still can live even with the illness."

Prayer

Gracious Christ, author of wisdom, grant me the patience and the willingness to live without

*answers. Help me to cherish each day I am given
and to savor the goodness of the life I am living.*
Amen.

Practice

Beginning today, start keeping track of what you
savor in the life you are living with illness. Be specific. Name anything that comes to mind. (Often
we over-look the goodness that is somewhat ordinary; beginning to name it helps us notice more
of the goodness that coexists with the illness.)
My own list, this morning, includes Maggie, our
border collie, and Cuthbert and Leftovers, our
cats. Also included in this ongoing list of what
I savor are: the aroma and taste of coffee, the
roses blooming on the deck, e-mails from dear
friends, much-needed rain.

Your list will be as singular as your life.
Remember to savor as you move through your
day, and give thanks.

Day Fourteen

As for me, I am afflicted and in pain.

Psalm 69:31

Some years ago I read an article[3] by a woman who was learning to live with an autoimmune disease. She discovered that she had been trying to "pass" for healthy. In other words, the last thing she would let herself know was that she was afflicted and in pain.

It may be that the hardest movement for us in living with illness is the movement of admitting that we are ill. Only when we let ourselves know that truth can we begin to create balance and live in such a way that our life with illness is *life*. Allowing the truth of the limitations of the illness to delineate our daily patterns allows us to live the truth in love.

What would your life look like if you found a creative balance particular to the needs of your body? What if you found yourself able to live *with* the illness, with its particular necessities and boundaries? What if you were able to tell the truth, in prayer and to yourself, about your experience and your life?

Prayer

O Christ of Love and Truth, grant me the grace to let myself know the steps to take to honor the life You offer me. May my life with this illness be marked by honesty and prayer.
Amen.

Practice

Reflect on the adjustments required by living with your particular illness. What has been the easiest for you? What has been the hardest? How have you allowed yourself to accept the limitations the illness has presented? As you reflect, if you discover something that seems stuck, allow that to come to prayer. For example, "Gracious God, I know that I need to refrain from eating sugar in order to live with the diabetes. Help my appetite to change, and grant me the desire to honor the life that you have given me."

Day Fifteen

You strengthen me more and more;
you enfold and comfort me.

Psalm 71:21

Perhaps you have known someone whose soul emanates the strength of love, the strength of Christ. An older friend of mine comes to mind: a neurosurgeon, he has lived through his first wife's death from cancer and he daily witnesses death and suffering as he offers his surgical skill in the operating room. He is a man who knows that life is fragile and resilient, beautiful and startling. He has also walked with many families through the valley of the shadow of death.

When Christ strengthens us, enfolds us, comforts us, we grow in our capacity for endurance and perseverance in love. We become more able to walk with others in their suffering and grief. We are more inclined to see our own sorrows within the context of the sorrows of the whole human family.

Illness can offer peculiar gifts, strange gifts—gifts of souls growing stronger, of hearts softening and comforting. As you live with your own illness, may you be alert to Christ's offering of his own strength for your inner being so that planted in love and rooted in love you may grow up into his own life for the world.

Prayer

Ever merciful Christ, this day, and every day, may You strengthen my heart and soul so that I may receive your comfort and offer that same comfort to others.

Amen.

Practice

Recall someone who has been of great comfort to you as you have learned to live with illness. What qualities does that person's life exhibit? Give thanks for this person and reflect on your own ability to offer comfort. How might you extend comfort to another? Does anyone in particular come to mind? If so, begin by steadily and quietly praying for that other person, awaiting Christ's guidance. Perhaps you need to phone or e-mail or send a card to the person you are led to comfort. Perhaps, for the moment, you are called to steadfast prayer and intercession, respecting the vulnerability of another.

Day Sixteen

When my mind became embittered,
I was sorely wounded in my heart.

Psalm 73:21

Let's be honest. Sometimes living with illness embitters us. Sometimes we fall prey to resentment. Sometimes we wonder why it is that the illness has come to live with us, and not with somebody else. The bitter, resentful habit of mind leads to a wounded heart. The bitter, resentful habit of thought leads to a woeful lack of love.

When our son Bryan was receiving chemotherapy, our weeks were marked by regular visits to the oncologist's office. We became part of the

Tuesday morning community. Those patients and family members with regular Tuesday morning appointments came to know each other, to share wisdom and strength, humor and candy.

One older woman, Emma, had lived with her cancer for some time. She had come to the end of possible treatments and was, as she put it, "sailing along" until the cancer reappeared. She could have been bitter. She was not. She could have been a Pollyanna. She was not. Emma was a realist. She always told the gathered community, "I've been glad for my life. Be glad for yours."

We all fall prey to bitterness and resentment from time to time. That's why we need friends and family to remind us: be glad for your life. Remember there are many others who live with illness, and many of them may not have been blessed as richly as we have been with family and friends and material goods.

Prayer

Loving and gentle Christ, help me to notice my own bitterness. Let it not wound my soul. And if it does wound, may I trust in your gentle power to heal my heart and make it new.

Amen.

Practice

When has your experience of living with illness led to bitterness or resentment? How have you sought guidance? Who has been a friend and companion in those times of reckoning with these feelings? When bitterness or resentment arises, how do you recognize its presence? Does it manifest in your body or in your behavior? Compose a prayer of your own, either asking for help with bitterness and resentment, or giving thanks for being delivered from them.

Day Seventeen

*We give you thanks, O God, we give you
thanks, calling upon your Name
and declaring all your wonderful deeds.*

Psalm 75:1

My dad suffered a heart attack several years ago.
After having angioplasty and recovering from having his heart shocked back into rhythm, he began
reflecting on the "miracle" (as he called it) that he
was still alive. One day I found him at his desk,
doing some math. "What are you computing?"
I asked. "I am figuring out how many times my
heart has beat in my lifetime, more or less. I have
never thanked God for that. I've just taken it for
granted. In fact, I've never thanked God for every-
thing that still works, and I'm in my eighties!"

Dad taught me a good lesson that day. He had taken the time to give thanks, not only for coming through a very frightening episode, but also for all that had worked within his own body for so many years.

It is so easy for us to focus on what is wrong when we live with an illness or a condition. It is so easy for us to fail to give thanks for the organs and systems that do the work they have been given to do. And it is so easy for us to forget to support our own health by grateful practices that offer our bodies adequate rest, nutrition, exercise, and care.

This day, take the time to give thanks for all that works within your own body. Be specific: "Thank you for the blood that courses through these veins, taking needed nutrients to all my cells." "Thank you for these bones that hold up my flesh."

And in the days ahead, add to the thanksgivings, perhaps even writing them down each day.

Prayer

I give You thanks, most gracious God, for the gift of this embodied life, and for all of these organs, systems, and bones that continue to function, even with illness. Help me to honor the gift of this body that You have brought into being.

Amen.

Practice

Give thanks today for what is working within your body. Give thanks for the mysterious perseverance of organs and circulatory systems in the face of bodily disruption. Give thanks not only with prayer, but also by asking yourself what you might do to embody the thanksgiving. Maybe you could stretch your muscles or eat what your body needs or be faithful about your medicine regimen. Be creative in embodying the thanksgiving, and be concrete and specific. For example, if you live with diabetes, you might want to make a donation to an organization that helps those who cannot afford to buy insulin. If you live with cancer, you may want to embody your thanksgiving by taking good reading material to the oncologist's office.

DAY EIGHTEEN

You are the God who works wonders.

Psalm 77:14

Several years ago when I was on staff of a church here in San Antonio, during a staff meeting, we began reflecting on the fact that each one of us, had we lived one generation earlier, would probably have died at an early age. One of us had had malignant melanoma. Another had been in a terrible car accident and required extensive surgery. Another had almost lost a baby when things went wrong at delivery; an emergency C-section saved both mother and child.

We tend to forget that ours is an age of wonders. Laparoscopic surgeries prevent blood loss and shorten recovery time. Diagnostic tests catch all kinds of maladies at an early stage, thus allowing for better treatment. Physicians of all specialties bring stunning intellectual and intuitive capacities to the service of their patients.

In all of this, the God who works wonders *is* working. Divine grace and wisdom are inspiring research, diagnostic care, and ongoing medical attention for a full panoply of diseases and conditions. Remember to thank those who tend you. Remember to give thanks to God for your medicines, for the diagnostic tests that allow for a precise diagnosis, for the aides, the nurses, the technicians, the physicians whose dedication allows you to *live* with illness. And give thanks to God for the wonders worked in and through human memory, reason, and skill.

Prayer

I give You thanks, most gracious God, for the physicians, nurses, aides, and technicians whose skill and attention has been offered on my behalf. Grant me a deepening awareness of and gratitude for your working in and through their care and ministration.

Amen.

Practice

Call to mind the various physicians who have tended you as you have lived with your particular illness. Write their names in your journal, and give thanks for each one. Recall the nurses who have come to your aid. Write their names in your journal and give thanks for each one. Recall the lab technicians who have tended you or have taken blood samples. Write their names in your journal and give thanks (you may be noticing that you do not know all of their names—and yet these people have helped you continue to live, through their skill and experience). If you feel led to write to any of these people who have tended you, send them a card. And, if you sense it is appropriate, you may want to let their superiors know of a job well done. We are a society of complainers; one gift of living with illness is to be steadfast in naming gifts received and letting others know of your gratitude for work well done.

DAY NINETEEN

*He led them with a cloud by day, and all
the night through with a glow of fire.*

Psalm 78:14

This line from Psalm 78 recounts the experience
of the Israelites as they trekked through the wilderness of Sinai after having escaped from slavery
in Egypt. The living God led them, with a cloud
by day, and a pillar of fire by night. They had no
map. They had never been this way before. They
followed the cloud or the pillar of fire, through the
desert, searching for the land of milk and honey.

Sometimes when we live with illness we find we
are in territory for which we have no map. We discover, perhaps for the first time, that we can be truly

sick and weak. Or we may discover that a chronic condition has suddenly produced some unforeseen secondary effects. Or we find that a malady that was chronic has been pronounced terminal, confronting us with the fact of our mortality.

The imagery of the cloud by day and the pillar of fire by night invites us to be alert for God's presence with us in these times. We may not have a sign as clear as these. Yet God's presence is there with us when we do not know the way. When we have no compass. When we have no map. When we have no idea how a day will unfold. God is present through Christ in and through those times and those places. God is present within your broken body. God is present within each cell, within your breath, within your marrow.

And God is present in and through those who tend you, those who help you, those who walk with you.

Prayer

Ever-present Christ, when I don't know what will come next, when I don't know what the day will bring, when I cannot control my circumstances, may I remember that You are as near to me as my breath, as close to me as the beating of my heart. Amen.

Practice

Begin with finding a comfortable position, and then allow your breath to find its own gentle rhythm. You may find it helpful to breathe gently for several minutes. Then, if you are physically able, place one hand on your chest so that you can feel the beat of your heart. As you become aware of the steady beat, remember that God is closer to you than the beat of your heart. Let the prayer be nothing more than awareness of your heartbeat and awareness of God's presence.

DAY TWENTY

❧❀❧

So mortals ate the bread of angels;
he provided for them food enough.

Psalm 78:25

When the Israelites found themselves in the wilderness of Sinai, God gave them a kind of bread called manna for food. The manna would last only for a day, and it appeared as frost on the ground. Food for the journey. Food for the day. Food that was sufficient for their needs.

I like to know I have enough food for several days, if not for a week—whether that is food for the table or food for the spirit. I have trouble believing that if I have food for only one day, there will be food again the following day.

When our son Bryan was diagnosed with brain cancer, we learned to cherish food for the day. Initially, that food looked like good postoperative reports. And then it began to look like diminished swelling and good response to radiation. Later it looked like Bryan's happy participation in speech therapy and his steadily returning strength.

Then one day the cancer returned. We were in new territory. We had no map and we were completely out of hope, out of strategies to live with the cancer's return. Bryan himself gave us the food, his presence was manna enough. Later there would be days when we, his friends and family, gave him the manna. As Bryan became weaker, his friends sat with him. Family members told him stories and thanked him for all he had offered in his thirty-one years of life. Food sufficient for the day. Bread of hope, bread of life, bread of love—shared and received as we all lived with illness.

Prayer

O Christ, You are our bread and our sustenance. Grant me the grace this day to receive the bread of

*life and the food of hope that you offer. And may I
share this bread with those I meet along the way.
Amen.*

Practice

What kind of "bread" do you need this day?
Bread of friendship? Bread of solitude? Bread of
reassurance? Bread of nutrition? Reflect on what
kind of manna you need right now, in this present moment. Write a prayer asking for what you
need, and also remembering all those who have
that same need this day.

DAY TWENTY-ONE

How dear to me is your dwelling,
O Lᴏʀᴅ of hosts!

Psalm 84:1

Our bodies are the very dwelling place of God. Part
of the great "showing" that we receive in the birth,
life, death, and resurrection of Jesus is that God is
telling us that the divine life and matter are made
for each other. In Jesus, God lives a human life
from the inside out. That means that God shows
forth who God is *through a body*. Yes, Jesus had
headaches and indigestion and bone-deep fatigue.
He bled real blood and he felt real pain.

God cherishes your body as God's own dwelling. Your body is as dear to God as the body of

Jesus. Your body, even with its weakness and its difficulties, is a remarkable creation. And it is your body that allows you to be in this earthly existence in a particular way, knowing the world and those whom you love, experiencing this life in all its transitory beauty and mystery.

Imagine cherishing your body as God does. Imagine saying of your body this day, "How dear to me is your dwelling, O LORD of hosts!" Know that your body is indeed the very dwelling place of God, even if it is afflicted, even if you struggle from day to day. Deep within your very cells, deep within the very matter of your physical self, God in Christ dwells with you and makes a home there. So how could your body be anything *but* holy?

Prayer

Tender and loving God, may I ever remember that You cherish this dear body, broken as it may be. May I honor your presence within and remember that this body is your own creation, sustained in being by your own Spirit, and honored by your Christ.
Amen.

Practice

Begin by finding a comfortable position, and then slowly allow your breath to find its own rhythm. When you have been breathing gently, focusing on the breath for several minutes, add this prayer:

You make your home (inhalation)
In this body. (exhalation)

Stay with the prayer as long as you wish. When you sense the time of prayer has come to its natural end, offer a simple thanksgiving.

DAY TWENTY-TWO

~❧~

*Happy are the people whose
strength is in you! whose hearts are
set on the pilgrims' way.*

Psalm 84:4

In the first generations of Christianity, before the religion was known by that name, the faithful who began to follow the Risen Christ spoke of the Way (Acts 9:2). From the beginning, followers knew that Christ had called them to walk as companions, and to practice what Jesus had taught and lived. Those early Christians also understood that life itself is a journey, a pilgrimage, a way to be walked.

So, too, with illness. We walk a way, a pilgrimage, through living with a physical or mental condition.

Any of us who have made a walking trip or have had the experience of a walking pilgrimage, know that companions help us keep going. Rhythms of conversation and silence form community. Shared experience and memory bind us together.

As you make your own pilgrimage with illness, give thanks for those who walk with you. These may be friends who never miss a step. Or they may be companions for a day who appear suddenly in a waiting room or a treatment center. They may be others who live with the same illness that you do.

Our inner strength is confirmed and renewed by our pilgrim companions—those whose presence enlivens our journey, even when we are gravely ill. Our inner strength is blessed and upheld by Christ in his many different disguises[4] as he walks with us, accompanying us on our way through these holy companions.

Prayer

As I walk this pilgrim path through illness, grant me, O Christ, companions for the journey. And may I be a companion to others in return, remem-

bering that by sharing our life and our experience, we lean on your strength as we abide in one another.

Amen.

Practice

Give thanks for those companions on the path of living with illness who have walked with you along the way: those who are steady friends, those who have appeared when you needed them, those who have handed on wisdom for living with your particular illness, those who have given you hope, those who have prayed for you from afar. Then pray for all those who live with your particular illness, and who may not have companions for their journey.

DAY TWENTY-THREE

※⟡※

Those who go through the desolate valley will find it a place of springs.

Psalm 84:5

Occasionally, when living with illness has been a dry and dusty road, lonely in the extreme and fraught with fear and anxiety, we come upon an oasis. We find a place of springs, a way station where we may drink of hope and community. This is not to say we have found a cure. It is to say that sometimes, unbidden, we find ourselves in circumstances that offer respite and gentle mercy.

We might miss the offering of respite because we have become so habituated to simply slogging through, day by day. We might miss the early sun casting intricate patterns on the wall, or the dog's soft wuffling slumber. We might miss the savor of that first cup of coffee or the refreshing sight of a red-tailed hawk in the pecan tree.

When living with illness has become a hard journey, sometimes we can choose to seek respite. Sometimes we can find a way to breathe through the hardest spots, to notice something of beauty and grace in the midst of the most difficult circumstances.

A friend of mine was recently hospitalized for the treatment of her condition. In the middle of the night, when it was time for her blood to be drawn, the phlebotomist appeared. He entered the room gently, and turned on a low light that was sufficient for his work but not glaring. He moved kindly and softly. He found the vein on the first try (thank God!), and left as gently as he had entered. She felt as if she had had a little oasis, a moment of human contact that, while efficient, was also profoundly marked by respect and mercy.

Notice the springs of water on your journey. Notice those moments when beauty appears.

Notice when mercy and kindness greet you unexpectedly. Notice, receive, and drink deeply from those springs.

Prayer

O Christ, you offer living water through your promise of life and hope. May I be aware of the springs in this desolate valley, and may I receive the refreshment You offer my soul and spirit.

Amen.

Practice

Recall a time when you have unexpectedly been offered a drink of mercy and hope. Who offered you a drink from the "place of springs"? How was it offered? How did you receive the offering? Give thanks for the offering. Begin to notice and give thanks as you journey with the illness.

DAY TWENTY-FOUR

Do you work wonders for the dead?

Psalm 88:11

From time to time the voice we hear in the psalms takes us aback. This verse, "Do you work wonders for the dead?," is not the customary way that most of us address God. I don't know about you, but I was socialized not to ask this kind of question of God. For heaven's sake, when we are praying we need to be on our best behavior, right?

The ancient Hebrews would tell us we have it all wrong. The voice we hear in the psalms tells God just how hard life is at times. Occasionally we come across a line that will provide strength for this pilgrimage of living with illness: "How long, O LORD?" (Ps. 13:1) or "Have mercy upon us, O LORD, have mercy, for we have had more than enough of contempt" (Ps. 123:4).

Today we hear from Psalm 88 a line that almost taunts God. "Do you work wonders for the dead?"

Can you imagine allowing yourself to be that honest with God? Years ago my spiritual director said to me, "Mary, if you think that God will disappear in the face of your hurt and your questions, then that is not God." That counsel, and the example of the bald honesty we find in the psalms, has led me to rail at God from time to time about my own illness, about Bryan's cancer, about the terrible afflictions that many endure.

As my director pointed out, speaking the truth that is in my heart and soul allows for a true and deep relationship in prayer to develop. When I only pray what I think God wants to hear, I miss this truth: God already knows what is in my heart and is well familiar with my despair, my fear, my anger, my fragile faith.

Prayer

Gracious God, grant me the grace to tell You the truth, to trust You enough to let anger and fear come to speech and be transformed. May I remember that You know me better than I can know myself.

Amen.

Practice

Choose one fear or hurt or anger that you have not laid before God in prayer. Trust that in the ancient tradition of the Hebrew psalms, you may speak that into being. Trust that God will not disappear in the face of your saying what you need to say—and what is already known to this loving God in whom we live and move and have our being. Trust that God is infinitely merciful, and will not leave you in the face of your fear or hurt or anger. Let the prayer be real. Let the speech be as raw as it needs to be.

If you perceive that you need a spiritual friend or director to be with you in this practice, wait to try it until you can be in the presence of that person.

Day Twenty-five

⁂

*Lord, you have searched me out
and known me; you know my sitting
down and my rising up; you discern
my thoughts from afar.*

Psalm 139:1

When we live with illness, there is a lot of sitting down, and some rising up. There is a lot of lying down, and some rising up. In all of those movements, both physical and spiritual, God is with us. In all of those wild swings of hope and disappointment, relief and shock, highs and lows, sittings and risings, God is with us. In every twist and turn, in every improvement and decline, God embraces the fullness of our life, whatever our malady may be.

This God who is with us will not let us go. Sometimes it certainly feels as if we have been abandoned by God—though the longer I live, and the longer I live with illness, the more often I find that what looks like abandonment may in reality be deepening intimacy and trust. I have found that old images of God have been shattered, and that God is offering a new dimension to the relationship in prayer.

How can that be? Life shatters my various ways of trying to put God in a box. This is not to deny my own confusion or sadness or fear. It is to say that part of me, from time to time, still wants for there to be a ready solution. Part of me wants that fix-it "god." Part of me wants the magic wand to make things dandy all over again.

The mystery of God, revealed through Jesus, is that God embraces and indwells every bit of our human frailty. God may be found more truly when our bodies are compromised. This is not to say that God gives us illness so that we can be tested. This is not to say that God makes us sick so that we can learn something.

It is far more mysterious, more intimate, beyond human comprehension. The Christian witness is that God indwells our life with divine Life. God is present in and through all that we experience. Even when we least feel it, least experience it, God is there.

Prayer

Gracious God, You are with me in all times and in all places. There is no place where You are not. There is no part of my being that is outside the realm of your love. Grant me the capacity to trust in your presence and your love.

Amen.

Practice

Begin with a position that is comfortable for you, and allow your breath to find its own gentle rhythm. Breathe gently for several minutes. Then imagine that you are being held gently, surely, steadily by Christ. (Since, as Mother Teresa of Calcutta put it, Christ has many different disguises, allow Christ to come to you as Christ desires, in a way that might surprise you.) Notice how your body responds to being held by Mercy larger than you, far larger than your illness. Rest in this presence for as long as you desire. When you sense that the prayer is complete, give thanks and return your attention to your breath.

Day Twenty-six

❧

You trace my journeys and my resting-places
and are acquainted with all my ways.

Psalm 139:2

Sometimes it makes me smile to imagine that God
is acquainted with all my ways. God knows that
I sing to my border collie. And God knows that I
love the aroma of newly turned earth in the spring.
God knows I am a Texan through and through
and that I love speaking Spanish.

And God knows that my way through illness
is an odd journey. No one besides me and God
knows what this body feels like from the inside
out. No one besides me and God knows the subtle
signs of trouble that can be addressed or ignored

(to my peril). No one besides me and God is acquainted with my inner conversation about the many daily decisions that might—or might not—support my healing.

One of our struggles is the deepening realization that God in Christ is far more intimate with us than we ever dreamed. It easier to reject a God I can hold at arm's length. It is easier to walk away from that false "Old Man in the Sky" or from "The Great Accountant" or from "The God Who Sends Us to Hell."

What if all of that is false? What if every one of those images is nothing more than a puff of wind, a bit of smoke, a passing illusion? What if this God who knows me intimately, knows this illness, is indeed acquainted with all my ways, and cherishes the singularity of my life as God's own creation? What if it truly is all about a love that we can barely imagine?

Prayer

Gentle Christ, You know me through and through and in that knowing You offer love and delight, mercy and wisdom. As I walk with this illness, may I remember that You know well each detail, each aspect, each moment of my life, and that you encircle me with your presence.

Amen.

Practice

For today, take as truth the psalmist's assertion that God is "acquainted with all my ways." What are some of your daily, mundane ways that God is acquainted with? What patterns and rhythms of your ordinary life tell you and God who you are, how you cherish the life you are living (or not), and what matters the most to you at this time?

Day Twenty-seven

⁂

Where can I go then from your Spirit?
where can I flee from your presence?
If I climb up to heaven, you are there;
if I make the grave my bed,
you are there also.

Psalm 139:6–7

Living with illness takes us into places and situations that can be harrowing. Some of us live through complicated surgeries. Others endure the steady diminishment of physical or mental capacity. Others struggle to live with a condition that has no cure.

The assurance of our faith is this: there is no place, no circumstance, where God is not present. There is no place where the Spirit of God does not breathe. There is no place in which God chooses not to be.

A friend of mine who has lived with a lot of loss and illness in her family says this: "If God isn't telling us in Jesus that all of this is held in God's embrace, then I am out of here."

I love her honesty. I love her ability to take the experiences she has lived with—some of them so distressing—and state that in those experiences, God is there. She is not someone given to saccharine versions of faith. Her life has been too hard. She has shaken her fist at God and cried out. She has felt sad and abandoned. And over the years, she has learned that God is with her, in all the dyings and risings of her life.

Prayer

Help me, when I do not see or understand, to trust in your presence, O Christ. Help me, when my body hurts and my spirit fails, to know that I am in your hands. Help me, when the circumstance of illness breaks my heart, to know that You weep with me.

Amen.

Practice

Recall a moment in your life with illness when you have felt no one else understood or felt as you have. Return to that moment in your memory. As you do so, see that Christ is there with you, both in the way you remember the moment and in the way that moment was actually lived. How do you respond to Christ's presence with you?

DAY TWENTY-EIGHT

*Darkness is not dark to you;
the night is as bright as the day;
darkness and light to you are both alike.*

Psalm 139:11

In the early years of Christianity, Jesus was identified as the Light of God. This Light is beyond the brightness of the sun. This is the Great Uncreated Light that brought forth the lesser lights of the universe. Not one subatomic particle has been made without this Light. Each of us comes forth from this Light, and in time each of us will return to the Light that is our home.

In the tradition of the Christian East, the theologians speak of God's "dazzling darkness."

By this they mean that the Great Light is so bright that when we gaze at it, our understanding may be "darkened." This is not a darkness of ignorance and sin but one caused by the stunning illumination of God's presence. We discover how much we do not know. We discover that God is so much more than we had thought or imagined. We discover that we are so little, so dependent—and yet so cherished.

We are ever in Christ who is the Light, the Gracious Light and Pure Brightness. When our personal journeys enter a time of grief or despair, our darkness is always held by that Great Light. As we grow in a deepening awareness of this uncreated Light, may the darker days of our journey be infused with that Light. And may we celebrate the eternal hope that Christ, the Light of the world, gives so graciously.

Prayer

O Gracious Light, O Christ, enlighten my days and my nights with your mercy. Illumine the lives of all who suffer with your consolations. May

we ever remember that we come from your own
uncreated Light and will be welcomed home at
our end.

Amen.

Practice

Notice today the various ways in which light is
present in your life—through the sun or lightbulbs
or stars. Notice all the ways in which light changes
your experience of where you live. Remember
that the Uncreated Light is far greater than any
of these lights. Remember that the Uncreated
Light brought you into being. Remember that the
Uncreated Light is Love, from which we come and
to which we return.

If you wish, pray these ancient words:

O Gracious Light, pure brightness of the
everliving Father in heaven.[5]

DAY TWENTY-NINE

*I will thank you because
I am marvelously made; your works
are wonderful and I know it well.*

Psalm 139:13

Yes, even when we live with illness, we are marvelously made. Even when we have daily struggles with bodies that are laboring to continue, we are crafted by divine skill and patience.

Living with illness can distort our souls if we allow it. Living with illness can lead us to be small-souled and mean-spirited. It is no small feat to grow in love and mercy while living in pain. And yet you and I both know people whose hearts have grown beyond measure despite living with illness. We know people whose lives have become increasingly marked by compassion even as their bodies are afflicted.

Our souls grow larger, becoming truly magnanimous, as we practice gratitude. Can you still breathe? Give thanks for that. Can you still digest? Give thanks for that. Can you still move your limbs? Give thanks that you have them.

And then take it one step further. Recognize fully that you are marvelously made. Notice that there is physical evidence that you are marvelously made. Notice the beauty, the intricacy, the stunning transformative possibilities of your own body. Notice and remember that you did not bring yourself into being. Not your heart, not your lungs, not your bones, not your toenails. Each part of you was fashioned by God.

Remember and give thanks. Much care has been lavished on the creation of each one of us embodied souls. The Spirit of God who brought you into being will receive you at the end, in freedom and grace.

Prayer

Gracious Christ, I thank you that I am marvelously made. I thank you that this body works as well as it does, despite the challenges of the illness with which I live.

Amen.

Practice

Begin by gently paying attention to your breath. Then, as you are ready, look at one of your hands (or choose another part of your body). Behold your hand with love. Notice every line, every vein, every crease. Notice anything that makes your hand distinctively your hand. If you wish, trace your hand on a piece of paper. Remember that the lines of your hand are truly unique; no one else has those lines, those fingerprints. Your hand reflects the handiwork of God, the singular creative work of the Light from whom you come.

Give thanks for being marvelously made, and pray for those whose hands have helped you along the way in your illness.

DAY THIRTY

My body was not hidden from you,
while I was being made in secret.

Psalm 139:14

Our bodies were not hidden from God when we
were being knit together in our mother's womb.
Our bodies were not hidden from God as we
entered earthly life and began to be (as the Celtic
tradition puts it) "guests of the world." Our bodies were not hidden from God when illness came
to be a permanent resident in our lives.

Indeed, we are ever held in the kindly gaze of
love. God in Christ sees and knows our physical
afflictions. God in Christ walks with us to the

doctor's office, to the hospital, to the chemotherapy treatment, to the surgical suite.

In the depths of your being, right now, this day, God in Christ abides. In the depths of your soul, God in Christ intimately knows the pattern of your days and the disruptions of your illness. In the depths of your cells, so carefully crafted and so lovingly designed, this God who is your Source and your End participates and knows all that you endure, all that you hope for, all that you live with.

May you rest in that assurance, and receive every consolation that Christ has to offer.

Prayer

Gracious Christ, may I ever remember that I am not hidden from You, and that whether I know it or not, You are with me every step of the way.

Amen.

Practice

As you journey this day with your illness, and journey in the days ahead, offer this prayer from the Celtic tradition:

> *My walk this day with God,*
> *My walk this day with Christ,*
> *My walk this day with Spirit,*
> *The Threefold all-kindly:*
> *Ho! Ho! Ho! The Threefold all-kindly.*
> (from the *Carmina Gadelica*[6])

Afterword

*I will thank you because
I am marvelously made.*

Psalm 139:13

Some years ago a friend of mine who is a rabbi observed that he thinks the essence of our prayer is "thanks" and "help," in that order. His point was that Judaism recognizes that all life, even life marked by the presence of illness, is a gift. All of our days are a gift. Our bodies, even when compromised, are a wonder. Each organ works without our conscious input—lungs breathe, hearts pump, bones uphold, livers and kidneys cleanse and filter.

Most of the time we take all of this for granted. We only notice the wonder and gift of our bodies when something goes wrong. We fail to give thanks for our bodies until we are frustrated or angered by illness or aging.

The Jewish sages would tell us we have missed the point. They would point us to the regular practice of giving thanks for our first breath at birth and our first breath of each waking day. They would even remind us to be grateful for properly working bowels!

As you come to the end of these meditations and practices, may you begin to offer thanksgiving, and then ask for help. May your thanksgivings be as regular, ordinary, and specific as the constraints of your illness demand: "I give thanks that all my organs are working in the face of chemotherapy and radiation." "Thank you for a heart that continues to beat steadily after surgery." "Thank you for lungs that still function despite the cystic fibrosis."

This way of prayer is not saccharine. This is a way of thanking while being completely honest and clear about the context of the illness and its limitations.

After thanksgiving and praise, move to "help." You may ask for help through a procedure, help in gaining strength, help in preparing to die. Ask for what you need, not for what you think you are supposed to ask for. Start with being honest. Start with telling the truth.

And may the gracious and ever-living God who has received your prayers make known to you the infinite Mercy and Compassion that uphold you and grant you peace.

Amen.

Notes

1. See Sheldon Vanauken, *A Severe Mercy* (New York: HarperOne, 1987).

2. Thomas Keating, *Foundations for Centering Prayer and the Christian Contemplative Life* (New York: Continuum, 2002), 203.

3. Rabbi Susan Schnur, "Is Our Suffering Transformative?," *Lillith* (Winter 1996): 12–13.

4. Eileen Egan, "Polar Opposites?: Remembering the Kindred Spirits of Dorothy Day and Mother Teresa," *Catholic Peace Voice* (Fall 1997), 3.

5. "O Gracious Light," The Book of Common Prayer (New York: Church Hymnal Corporation, 1979), 118.

6. Alexander Carmichael, *Carmina Gadelica: Hymns and Incantations* (Edinburgh: Lindisfarne Press, 1992), 203.

www.ingramcontent.com/pod-product-compliance
Lightning Source LLC
Jackson TN
JSHW011411130125
77033JS00024B/961